PIZZAS & PASTA

TARLA DALAL

India's # 1 cookery author

SANJAY & CO.
BOMBAY

CREDITS

Fifth Printing 2004
Copyright © Sanjay & Co.
ISBN No. 81-86469-32-X

Price : **Rs. 89/-**

Published & Distributed by :
SANJAY & COMPANY
353/A-1, Shah & Nahar Industrial Estate,
Dhanraj Mill Compound, Lower Parel (W), Mumbai-400 013. INDIA.
Tel. : (91-22) 2496 8068 ● Fax : (91-22) 2496 5876
E-mail : sanjay@tarladalal.com

Research & **Production Design** PINKY CHANDAN ARATI KAMAT JYOTI SHROFF	**Designed by** S. KISHOR	**Photography** VINAY MAHIDHAR **Food Styling** NITIN TANDON

Printed by : **JUPITER PRINTS**, Mumbai.

OTHER BOOKS BY TARLA DALAL

INDIAN COOKING
Tava Cooking
Rotis & Subzis
Desi Khana
The Complete Gujarati Cook Book
Mithai
Chaat
Achaar aur Parathe
The Rajasthani Cookbook
Swadisht Subzian [New]

WESTERN COOKING
The Complete Italian Cookbook
The Chocolate Cookbook
Eggless Desserts
Mocktails & Snacks
Soups & Salads
Mexican Cooking
Easy Gourmet Cooking
Chinese Cooking
Easy Chinese Cooking
Thai Cooking
Sizzlers & Barbeques [New]

TOTAL HEALTH
Low Calorie Healthy Cooking
Pregnancy Cookbook
Baby and Toddler Cookbook
Cooking with 1 Teaspoon of Oil
Home Remedies
Delicious Diabetic Recipes
Fast Foods Made Healthy
Healthy Soups & Salads [New]
Healthy Breakfast [New]

MINI SERIES
A new world of Idlis & Dosas
Cooking under 10 minutes
Fun Food for Kids
Roz Ka Khana
Microwave - Desi Khana
T.V. Meals
Paneer [New]
Parathas [New]
Chawal [New]

GENERAL COOKING
Exciting Vegetarian Cooking
Party Cooking
Microwave Cooking
Quick & Easy Cooking
Saatvik Khana
Mixer Cook Book

The Pleasures of Vegetarian Cooking
The Delights of Vegetarian Cooking
The Joys of Vegetarian Cooking
Cooking With Kids
Snacks Under 10 Minutes
Ice-Cream & Frozen Desserts
Desserts Under 10 Minutes [New]

INDEX

PIZZAS

PIZZAS

PASTA

PASTA SOUPS AND SALADS

PASTA MAIN COURSES

PIZZAS

THE STORY OF PIZZA

Although there is much speculation about the origin of the pizza, it is usually associated with the old Italian city of Naples. It was then simple street food, which was richly flavoured and quickly made. It was not always round and flat as we know it today, but was folded up like a book with filling inside. It was sold on the streets and was eaten by the working man and his family.

*The word "Pizza" actually means a kind of **pie**. The classic "Neapolitan" Pizza, the best known of the many varieties, consists of a thin crust dough topped with fresh tomato sauce, mozzarella cheese and a sprinkling of oregano. Another classic is the "Margherita" pizza, named after the Italian Queen Margherita. On a visit to Naples, Queen Margherita requested for a local speciality. She was served a pizza in the colours of the Italian flag - red tomatoes, green basil and white Mozzarella. The Queen was delighted and the dish was given her name.*

The Americans have adopted the pizza, glorified it and raised it to a place of honour in their national cuisine. Apart from being popular, few other dishes are as versatile as the pizza with its several combinations of bases and toppings which can be served to suit every palate and every occasion.

*Although pizzas are readily available in the neighbourhood pizzeria, they never seem to taste as good as a real home-made pizza. A home-made pizza is a thing of beauty. **It may seem complicated the first time you make one, but it becomes very easy from then on.***

To get the best from your home-made pizza, use only fresh ingredients and buy the best.

COMMONLY USED INGREDIENTS

CHEESE

a. **Mozzarella** - *This cheese has a soft texture, it is mild white and has a delicate flavour. It can be used for salads and provides a tangy layer in baked dishes. It is also a popular topping for pizzas for its ability to melt and to produce strings of cheese once a pizza is baked and a slice is cut apart.*

b. **Parmesan** - *A mature, hard cheese. Excellent for topping on pasta. It is also used classically as an ingredient of pesto.*

c. **Processed Cheese** - *It is a "pasteurised cheese" (generally a blend of one or more cheeses of the same variety or two or more varieties) which is readily available in the market. Use in any recipe, stating "cheese" or "table cheese".*

d. **Cheddar Cheese** - *One of the most popular and well known cheeses of the world which is made from cow's milk. It can be white or yellow in colour and is hard and smooth in texture. It imparts a good flavour to pasta recipes and can be used as a substitute for Parmesan cheese.*

e. **Cooking Cheese** - *A variety of cheese which is a blend of two or more cheeses in varying proportions, it is blended so as to melt readily while cooking.*

f. **Cheese Spread** - *It is a kind of processed cheese used as a topping for several recipes. It is available in several flavours like plain, garlic, pepper, cumin etc.*

g. **Flavoured Cheese** - *This includes an array of cheeses available at gourmet stores like herb flavoured cheeses, paprika cheese, pepper cheese, garlic cheese, cumin flavoured cheese.*

These can be made at home by mixing the desired

*flavouring ingredients like paprika, garlic etc.
with mozzarella or processed cheese.*

OLIVE OIL
*Olive oil which is the heart of so many Italian dishes has its
own characteristic flavour which enhances and complements
several pizza and pasta recipes. Olive oil is sold under various
classifications - "Virgin" (extra fine or fine) or "Pure"
(i.e. mixed virgin and refined olive oil)*

*However, olive oil can be substituted with refined oil in case
of non-availability.*

YEAST
*Two types of yeast are available in the market - fresh and
dried. Both types can be used for making of pizza bases. Fresh
yeast should always be stored in an airtight container and
refrigerated. Whenever dried yeast is used, it should be half
the quantity of fresh yeast mentioned in the recipe. As it is a
more concentrated yeast, it also needs to be activated in
lukewarm water or milk before using in a recipe.*

BASIL
*Basil belongs to the 'tulsi' family. It is available in dried form
or as fresh basil leaves which are packed and sold by some
vegetable vendors. If you use dried basil, use only half the
quantity specified in the recipe as dried herbs are more
concentrated.*

OREGANO
*Also known as wild marjoram, it is available in two forms -
fresh and dried. Dried oregano is very concentrated and
stronger in flavour and should be used sparingly. It combines
very well in Italian cooking in pasta and pizza sauces,
especially tomato based dishes.*

PARSLEY
*A family of aromatic herbs, used to flavour and garnish
several recipes. The most commonly available kind of parsley*

has flat smooth leaves and the other is the curled parsley which has bright green leaves and is used mostly as a garnish. It is available both in dried and fresh form. Fresh parsley is sold in packets by some vegetable vendors. Coriander is a part of the parsley family.

JALAPENO CHILLIES
A pickled variety of a large green Mexican chilli which is readily available at many grocery stores, pickled in vinegar.

THYME
A herb which belongs to the mint family. The leaves are used in fresh or dry form. It is highly aromatic and should therefore be used sparingly. Leaves of ajwain can be used as substitute for thyme.

CHILLI FLAKES
Chilli flakes are made from dried red chillies which are roughly pounded to form chilli flakes. The seeds of the chillies are removed before grinding the chillies. Chilli flakes or paprika flakes are readily available at grocery shops.

PINENUTS (CHILGOZA)
They are the small edible seeds of the stone pine. They can be eaten raw, but are usually roasted for using in recipes. In India, they are used for garnishes. Pinenuts are also used for making the pesto but can be substituted by walnuts in case of non-availability.

SEASONING CUBE
This consists of salt and artificial flavours and seasoning. It is easily available at all grocery stores and is an alternative to making stocks for soups.

MIXED HERBS
There are several recipes indicating the use of mixed dried herbs. It consists of equal proportions of dried oregano, thyme, basil and parsley mixed together. The mixture can be prepared or can be bought as mixed herbs from grocery shops.

PIZZA CRUSTS

BASIC PIZZA BASE

Makes 2 bases.

2 cups plain flour (maida)
2 teaspoons (10 grams) fresh yeast, crumbled
1 teaspoon sugar
1 tablespoon olive oil or oil
1 teaspoon salt

1. Combine all the ingredients except the olive oil in a bowl and knead into a soft dough using enough water until it is smooth and elastic.
2. Add the olive oil and knead again.
3. Cover the dough with a wet muslin cloth and allow it to prove till it doubles in volume (approx 15 to 20 minutes).
4. Press the dough lightly to remove the air.
5. Divide the dough into 2 equal parts.
6. Roll each portion into a circle of 250 mm. (10") diameter and 6 mm. (¼") thickness.
   Use as required.

- *Fresh yeast can be easily purchased from your local bakery in small quantities.*
- *You can also use half the quantity of dry yeast instead of fresh yeast for the above recipe and follow the instructions on the packet.*
- *You can also use a ready pizza base for any pizza.*

VARIATIONS:
HERB PIZZA BASE

Add 1 teaspoon of mixed dried herbs and 1 teaspoon of chilli flakes to the above recipe at step 1.

SEEDED DOUGH

Add 2 tablespoons of sesame seeds and 2 tablespoons of poppy seeds to the above recipe at step 1. The seeds have to be toasted.

SWEET DOUGH

Add ¼ cup of granulated sugar to the above recipe at step 1 and reduce the salt to ½ teaspoon.

Note :
These pizza bases can be topped with your favourite toppings.

WHOLE MEAL BASE

This healthy pizza base packs in the goodness of whole wheat flour.

Makes 2 bases.

2 cups whole wheat flour (gehun ka atta)
2 teaspoons (10 grams) fresh yeast, crumbled
1 teaspoon sugar
2 tablespoons olive oil or oil
1 teaspoon salt

1. *Combine all the ingredients except the olive oil in a bowl and knead into a soft dough using enough water until it is smooth and elastic.*
2. *Add the olive oil and knead again.*
3. *Cover the dough with a wet muslin cloth and allow it to prove till it doubles in volume (approx 15 to 20 minutes).*
4. *Press the dough lightly to remove the air.*
5. *Divide the dough into 2 equal parts.*
6. *Roll each portion into a circle of 250 mm. (10") diameter and 6 mm. (¼") thickness.*
   Use as required.

POLENTA BASE

An innovative base made using the polenta. Polenta is a cornmeal porridge that is the traditional dish of Northern Italy.

Makes 2 bases.

For the polenta
6 tablespoons maize flour (makai ka atta)
½ teaspoon chilli powder
2 teaspoons butter
salt to taste

Other ingredients
1½ cups plain flour (maida)
2 teaspoons (10 grams) fresh yeast, crumbled
1 teaspoon sugar

For the polenta
1. Put ¾ cup of water to boil along with the butter, chilli powder and salt.
2. When the water boils, add the maize flour and mix well with a wooden spoon or whisk.
3. Cook for some time on a low flame, whisking continuously all the time till the mixture thickens.
4. Remove from the fire and cool.

How to proceed

1. Sieve the flour, add the prepared polenta, yeast, sugar and enough water to make a soft dough. Knead till it is smooth and elastic.
2. Cover with a wet muslin cloth and allow it to prove till it doubles in volume (approx 15 to 20 minutes).
3. Press the dough lightly to remove the air.
4. Divide the dough into 2 equal parts.
5. Roll each portion into a circle of 250 mm. (10") diameter and 6 mm. (¼") thickness.

   Use as required.

- Maize flour is made by coarsely milling dried corn. Maize flour or cornmeal is coarse, grainy and pale yellow in texture.

Top: *Deep Dish Farmer's Harvest; page 27*
Bottom: *Corn, Basil and Fusilli Soup; page 59*

5 GRAIN BASE

A nutritious alternative for the regular refined flour base.

Makes 2 bases.

¼ cup maize flour (makai ka atta)
¼ cup jowar flour
¼ cup millet flour (bajre ka atta)
¼ cup wholewheat flour (gehun ka atta)
1 cup plain flour (maida)
2 teaspoons (10 grams) fresh yeast, crumbled
1 teaspoon sugar
1 tablespoon olive oil or oil
1 teaspoon salt

1. Combine all the ingredients except the olive oil in a bowl and knead into a soft dough using enough water until it is smooth and elastic.
2. Add the olive oil and knead again.
3. Cover the dough with a wet muslin cloth and allow it to prove till it doubles in volume (approx 15 to 20 minutes).
4. Press the dough lightly to remove the air.
5. Divide the dough into 2 equal parts.
6. Roll each portion into a circle of 250 mm. (10") diameter and 6 mm. (¼") thickness.
   Use as required.

Top: *Thai Pizza; page 28*
Bottom: *Primavera Salad; page 62*

BASIC SAUCES

TOMATO SAUCE

A classic Italian recipe.

Preparation time: 10 minutes.
Cooking time: 25 to 30 minutes.
Makes approx. 1 cup.

4 large tomatoes
2 bay leaves
4 to 6 peppercorns
1 small onion, chopped
1 teaspoon garlic, chopped
½ capsicum, deseeded
2 tablespoons tomato purée (optional)
¼ cup tomato ketchup
1 teaspoon sugar
½ teaspoon dried oregano
2 tablespoons olive oil or oil
salt to taste

1. *Blanch the tomatoes in boiling water.*
2. *Peel, cut into quarters and deseed the tomatoes.*
3. *Chop finely and keep the tomato pulp aside.*
4. *Heat the olive oil, add the bay leaves and peppercorns and sauté for a few seconds.*
5. *Add the onion, garlic and capsicum and sauté for a few minutes.*

6. *Add the tomato pulp and allow it to simmer for 10 to 15 minutes until the sauce reduces a little.*
7. *Add the tomato purée, ketchup, sugar and salt and simmer for some more time.*
8. *Finally, add the oregano and mix well. Remove the capsicum, bay leaves and peppercorns and discard.*
   Use as required.

VARIATION:
EASY TOMATO SAUCE

Use 5 large tomatoes and 3 teaspoons of sugar for the above recipe instead of using tomato ketchup and tomato purée.

● *You can make in advance large quantities of this sauce by multiplying the above recipe and refrigerate until required.*

PESTO

A traditional recipe with the distinct flavours of fresh basil, nuts, garlic and olive oil.

Preparation time: 5 minutes.
Cooking time: 5 minutes.
Makes ½ cup.

¼ cup pine nuts (chilgoza) or walnuts, chopped
2 cups fresh basil leaves, loosely packed
2 tablespoons olive oil
1 teaspoon chopped garlic
salt to taste

1. *Lightly roast the pine nuts. Cool completely.*
2. *Combine all the ingredients in a blender and blend into a smooth paste.*
   Use as required.

VARIATION:
CLASSIC ITALIAN PESTO

Add ¼ cup of parmesan cheese at step 2 and follow the same method.

- *If walnuts are used in the recipe, the first step can be omitted.*
- *Ready to use pesto is also available in bottles at gourmet stores.*

2

SUN-DRIED TOMATO PESTO

A modified version of the traditional Italian pesto for those who love sun-dried tomatoes.

Preparation time: 5 minutes.
No cooking.
Makes ½ cup.

¼ cup pine nuts (chilgoza) or walnuts, chopped
¼ cup sun-dried tomatoes, page 24, soaked
2 tablespoons olive oil
1 teaspoon, chopped garlic
1 teaspoon chilli powder
salt to taste

1. Lightly roast the pine nuts. Cool completely.
2. Combine all the ingredients in a blender and grind to a smooth paste.
   Use as required.

- If walnuts are used in the recipe, the first step can be omitted.
- If you use sun-dried tomatoes which are preserved in oil, do not add the olive oil as mentioned in the recipe.

SUN-DRIED TOMATOES

Picture on page 53

A great way to preserve tomatoes. Sun-dried tomatoes are salty, chewy and tangy in taste. They impart a unique flavour to pizza and pasta recipes.

Makes ¾ cup (100 grams).

2 kg. firm red tomatoes
4 tablespoons sea salt (khada namak)

1. Wash and wipe the tomatoes.
2. Cut the tomatoes into quarters.
3. Toss the tomatoes with the salt, place on a sieve and leave to dry under the sun.
4. When the sun sets, cover the sieve with a muslin cloth.
5. Repeat for 6 to 7 days till the tomatoes dry out completely.
6. Store the sun-dried tomatoes in an airtight container.
7. Soak in a little warm water for about 5 minutes and use as required.

● Sun-dried tomatoes are available dried or preserved in olive oil.

PIZZAS

ORIGINAL MARGHERITA

Queen Margherita's favourite recipe served in the colours of the Italian flag - red tomatoes, green basil and white mozzarella.

Preparation time: 10 minutes.
Cooking time: 40 minutes.
Makes 2 pizzas.

1 recipe basic pizza base, page 12
1 recipe tomato sauce, page 20
10 to 12 fresh basil leaves, roughly chopped
1 cup cooking cheese or mozzarella cheese, grated
2 tablespoons olive oil
butter or oil for greasing

1. *Place one pizza base on a greased baking tray.*
2. *Spread half the tomato sauce on the pizza base.*
3. *Sprinkle with half the basil leaves and cheese on top of the pizza.*
4. *Drizzle with half of the olive oil and bake in a preheated oven at 200°C (400°F) for 20 minutes or until the base is evenly browned.*
5. *Repeat with the remaining ingredients to make another pizza.*
   Serve hot.

SKILLET PIZZA WITH ASPARAGUS AND BABY CORN

This delicious pizza can be made within minutes without using an oven. Surprise all your guests !

Preparation time: 15 minutes.
Cooking time: 30 minutes.
Makes 2 pizzas.

1 recipe basic pizza base, page 12
1 recipe tomato sauce, page 20
1 can (400 grams) asparagus / fresh asparagus
2 cups sliced baby corn (blanched)
1½ cups cooking cheese or mozzarella cheese, grated
1 tablespoon olive oil or oil for cooking

1. *Heat half the olive oil in a non-stick pan over a low flame and place a pizza base on it.*
2. *Spread half the tomato sauce over the pizza base.*
3. *Drain the asparagus and roughly mash it with a fork. Spread half the mashed asparagus over the pizza.*
4. *Neatly arrange 1 cup of baby corn over the asparagus.*
5. *Top with half the cheese.*
6. *Cover the pan with a lid and cook on a very slow flame for 10 to 12 minutes or till the base is evenly browned.*
7. *Repeat with the remaining ingredients to make another pizza.*
   Serve hot.

- *The trick to making this pizza is to keep the flame sufficiently low so that the base does not burn while cooking.*

- *Any recipe for a pizza can be cooked on a skillet.*

DEEP DISH FARMER'S HARVEST

Picture on page 17

A thick crust pizza cooked in a deep pie dish with lots of toppings.

Preparation time: 15 minutes.
Cooking time: 25 minutes.
Makes 1 pizza.

½ recipe basic pizza base, page 12
½ recipe tomato sauce, page 20
butter or oil for greasing

To be combined into a topping
8 fresh mushrooms, blanched and sliced
8 black olives, sliced
½ cup red pepper, diced
¼ cup cooked sweet corn kernels
2 to 3 pickled jalapeno peppers, sliced
½ tomato, diced
1 small onion, sliced
1 tablespoon celery, sliced
¼ teaspoon mixed dried herbs or oregano
salt to taste

For baking

½ cup cooking cheese or mozzarella cheese, grated
1 tablespoon olive oil or oil

1. Roll out the pizza dough into a circle of 200 mm. (8") diameter and 8 mm. (1/3") thickness. Line a 150 mm. (6") greased pie dish with it.
2. Spread the tomato sauce over the base and fill with the topping.
3. Top with the cheese and finally drizzle the olive oil over it.
4. Bake in a preheated oven at 180°C (360°F) for about 20 minutes or until the base is evenly browned.
   Serve hot.

THAI PIZZA

Picture on page 18

A cheese free pizza with peanut butter and tomato sauce topped with sesame seeds and garlic flavoured mushrooms, spring onions, paneer, celery and capsicum.

Preparation time: 15 minutes.
Cooking time: 40 minutes.
Makes 2 pizzas.

1 recipe basic pizza base, page 12
butter or oil for greasing

For the tomato peanut sauce

1 recipe tomato sauce, page 20
2 tablespoons peanut butter
1 teaspoon soya sauce

For the mushroom topping

2 cups sliced mushrooms
2 teaspoons sesame seeds
2 teaspoons garlic, grated
2 cups chopped spring onions
¼ cup celery, sliced
½ cup red, yellow and green capsicum, diced
¼ cup paneer or tofu, diced
2 teaspoons soya sauce
1 tablespoon oil
salt and pepper to taste

For the tomato peanut sauce
1. Combine all the ingredients and bring to a boil.
2. Simmer till the sauce becomes smooth, adding water if required. Keep aside.

For the mushroom topping
1. Heat the oil and sauté the sesame seeds and garlic.
2. Add the mushrooms and sauté for 2 to 3 minutes.
3. Add the spring onions, celery, capsicum, paneer, soya sauce, salt and pepper and stir well.
4. Remove from the heat and keep aside.

How to proceed
1. Place one pizza base on a greased baking tray.
2. Spread half the tomato peanut sauce on top.
3. Top with half the mushroom topping and bake in a preheated oven at 200°C (400°F) for 15 minutes or till the base is evenly browned.
4. Repeat with the remaining ingredients to make one more pizza.
   Serve hot.

TEX-MEX PIZZA

A polenta base topped with spicy beans, peppers and cheese.

Preparation time: 20 minutes.
Cooking time: 1 hour.
Makes 2 pizzas.

For the base
1 recipe polenta base, page 15
butter or oil for greasing

For the spicy bean topping
½ cup red kidney beans (rajma), soaked overnight and drained
1 clove garlic, chopped
1 green chilli, chopped
1 large onion, chopped
1 cup chopped tomatoes
1 teaspoon coriander powder (dhania powder)
2 teaspoons cumin seed powder (jeera powder)
½ teaspoon chilli powder
2 tablespoons tomato purée
1 tablespoon oil
1 tablespoon butter
salt to taste

Other ingredients
1 cup capsicum, sliced
1 cup cooking cheese or mozzarella cheese, grated

For the spicy bean topping
1. Pressure cook the red kidney beans till they are slightly overcooked. Drain and keep aside.
2. Heat the oil and butter in a saucepan. Add the garlic, green chilli and onion and stir for some time.
3. Add the tomatoes, coriander powder, cumin seed powder, chilli powder and tomato purée and cook for 10 to 15 minutes till the oil separates.
4. Add the red kidney beans and salt and mix well. Simmer for 5 to 7 minutes, adding water if required. Keep aside.

How to proceed
1. Place one polenta base on a greased baking tray.
2. Spread half the spicy bean topping on it.
3. Top with half the capsicum and cheese.
4. Bake in a preheated oven at 200°C (400°F) for about 10 to 15 minutes or till the base is evenly browned.
5. Repeat with the remaining ingredients to make one more pizza.

Serve hot.

MEDITER-RANEAN PIZZA

A pesto flavoured creamy corn sauce topped with roasted bell peppers makes this a great combination.

Preparation time: 15 minutes.
Cooking time: 40 minutes.
Makes 2 pizzas.

1 recipe basic pizza base, page 12
butter or oil for greasing

To be mixed into a Corn Pesto sauce
1 cup cream style sweet corn (canned)
3 tablespoons Pesto, page 22
salt to taste

For the topping
1 yellow pepper
1 red pepper
1 tablespoon olive oil or oil
salt to taste

For baking
1 cup cooking cheese or mozzarella cheese, grated

For the topping
1. Lightly grease both the peppers with the olive oil and roast over an open flame till the skin is browned evenly. Cool completely.
2. Peel the skin off the roasted peppers and cut into thin strips.
3. Sprinkle salt and keep aside.

32

How to proceed

1. *Place one pizza base on a greased baking tray.*
2. *Spread half the Corn Pesto sauce over the base.*
3. *Top with half the roasted bell peppers.*
4. *Sprinkle half of the cheese on top.*
5. *Bake in a preheated oven at 200°C (400°F) for 10 to 15 minutes or till the base is evenly browned.*
6. *Make another pizza using the other pizza base and the remaining ingredients.*

   Serve hot.

GOURMET PIZZA

Picture on page 35

A 5 grain pizza base topped with sautéed leeks and cheese.

Preparation time: 15 minutes.
Cooking time: 40 minutes.
Makes 2 pizzas.

1 recipe 5 grain base, page 19
1 recipe tomato sauce, page 20
butter or oil for greasing

For the topping

2 cups leeks or spring onions, chopped
3 cloves garlic, chopped
a pinch of nutmeg
2 stuffed olives, sliced

1 tablespoon butter or oil
salt to taste

For baking
1 cup cooking cheese or mozzarella cheese, grated

For the topping
1. *Heat the butter in a saucepan.*
2. *Add the leeks, garlic, nutmeg, olives and salt and stir-fry for 3 to 4 minutes. Keep aside.*

How to proceed
1. *Place one pizza base on a greased baking tray.*
2. *Spread half the tomato sauce and half the topping on it.*
3. *Top with half of the grated cheese.*
4. *Bake in a preheated oven at 200°C (400°F) for 15 to 20 minutes or till the base is evenly browned.*
5. *Repeat with the remaining ingredients to make another pizza.*
   Serve hot.

Facing page: *Gourmet Pizza; page 33*

ORIENTAL PIZZA

A polenta pizza base topped with onion, capsicum and braised spicy pineapple.

Preparation time: 15 minutes.
Cooking time : 40 minutes.
Makes 2 pizzas.

1 recipe polenta base, page 15
1 cup tomato sauce, page 20
butter or oil for greasing

For the topping
1 cup canned pineapple, cubed
1 large onion, sliced
2 cloves garlic, chopped
1 teaspoon grated ginger
1 teaspoon chilli powder
2 teaspoons soya sauce
½ cup capsicum, diced
1 teaspoon butter
1 teaspoon oil
salt to taste

For baking
½ cup cooking cheese or mozzarella cheese, grated

Facing page: *Mini Fruit and Almond Pizzas; page 47*

For the topping
1. Heat the butter and oil in a saucepan and sauté the onion in it.
2. When the onion turns translucent, add the garlic, ginger and chilli powder and fry for some time.
3. Then add the soya sauce, capsicum, pineapple and salt and mix together.
4. Remove from the heat and keep aside.

How to proceed
1. Place one pizza base on a greased baking tray.
2. Spread half the tomato sauce on the base.
3. Top with half the topping and grated cheese and bake in a preheated oven at 200°C (400°F) for 15 minutes or till the base is evenly browned.
4. Repeat with the remaining ingredients to make one more pizza.

   Serve hot.

TANDOORI PANEER CALZONE

Picture on page 63

Pizza envelopes stuffed with a tangy Indian filling.

Preparation time: 20 minutes.
Cooking time: 30 minutes.
Makes 4 calzones.

1 recipe basic pizza base, page 12
1 teaspoon sesame seeds
butter for greasing and glazing

For the tandoori paneer filling
1 cup cottage cheese (paneer), cubed
¼ cup capsicum, diced
¼ cup tomatoes, deseeded and diced
¼ cup onions, chopped
1 tablespoon fresh cream
2 teaspoons butter

To be mixed into a marinade
¹/₃ cup fresh thick curds
1 teaspoon chilli powder
1 teaspoon dried fenugreek leaves (kasuri methi), roasted and powdered
2 teaspoons ginger-garlic paste
1 teaspoon garam masala powder
salt to taste

For the tandoori paneer filling

1. Marinate the paneer, capsicum and tomatoes in the marinade for about 30 minutes.
2. Heat the butter in a saucepan, add the onions and sauté for sometime.
3. Add the marinated paneer mixture and fresh cream and simmer for 3 to 5 minutes.
4. Remove from the fire and allow to cool.
5. Divide into 4 equal portions.

How to proceed

1. Divide the pizza crust dough into 4 equal portions.
2. Roll out each portion of the dough into a circle of 125 mm. (5") diameter and 6 mm. (1/4") thickness.
3. Put one portion of the filling on each circle.
4. Fold each circle to form a semicircle.
5. Seal the ends with the help of a fork. (refer to picture on page 63)
6. Place on a greased baking tray. Cover with a wet cloth and keep aside for 20 minutes.
7. Sprinkle sesame seeds on each Calzone.
8. Bake in a hot oven at 225°C (450°F) for 20 minutes, till golden brown.
9. Remove from the oven and brush with melted butter. Serve hot.

- You can also deep fry these Calzone instead of baking them (step 8). They must be fried over a medium flame till they are golden brown on both sides.

- You can make Calzone using your favourite fillers e.g. mushroom, corn, cheese, spinach etc.

CHEESY VEGETABLE PIZZA

A herb flavoured crust topped with sautéed vegetables and a cheese sauce.

Preparation time: 15 minutes.
Cooking time: 50 minutes.
Makes 2 pizzas.

1 recipe herb pizza base, page 13
½ recipe tomato sauce, page 20

For the vegetable topping
½ cup baby corn, sliced and blanched
½ cup carrots, diced and blanched
½ cup zucchini, diced and blanched (optional)
½ cup red peppers, sliced
½ cup celery, sliced
1 tablespoon butter
salt and pepper to taste

For the cheese sauce
2 tablespoons butter
1 tablespoon plain flour (maida)
¼ cup milk
½ cup grated cheese
salt and pepper to taste

Other ingredients
½ cup cooking cheese or mozzarella cheese, grated
oil or butter for greasing

For the vegetable topping

1. Heat the butter in a pan, add all the vegetables and sauté for 2 to 3 minutes.
2. Season with salt and pepper and keep aside.

For the cheese sauce

1. Heat the butter in a pan. Add the flour and cook for 1 minute.
2. Slowly add ½ cup of water, stirring continuously so that no lumps form.
3. Add the milk, cheese, salt and pepper and bring to boil.
4. Remove from the fire and keep aside.

How to proceed

1. Place one herb pizza base on a greased baking tray.
2. Spread half the cheese sauce on top of the base and then top with half the vegetables.
3. Spoon half the tomato sauce decoratively over the vegetables and then sprinkle ¼ cup of grated cheese on top.
4. Bake in a preheated oven at 200°C (400°F) for 20 minutes or till the base is evenly browned.
5. Repeat with the remaining ingredients to make another pizza.

   Serve hot.

● You can use any of your favourite vegetables in place of the ones listed above.

TOMATO CHEESE PIZZA

Picture on cover

An easy to make recipe that is an Italian favourite.

Preparation time: 10 minutes.
Cooking time: 40 minutes.
Makes 2 pizzas.

1 recipe basic pizza base, page 12
6 large ripe tomatoes, sliced
1½ cups cooking cheese or mozzarella cheese, sliced
6 to 8 black olives, deseeded (optional)
salt and pepper to taste
butter or oil for greasing

For serving
chilli flakes

1. Place one pizza base on a greased baking tray.
2. Arrange the tomato and cheese slices alternatively on the pizza base, overlapping over each other.
3. Sprinkle some salt and pepper and decorate with olives, if desired.
4. Bake in a preheated oven at 200°C (400°F) for 20 minutes or till the base is evenly browned.
5. Repeat with the remaining ingredients to make another pizza.
   Serve hot with chilli flakes.

● You can also sprinkle ½ teaspoon of mixed dried herbs over each pizza at step 3 and bake as specified.

WALNUT, APPLE AND FIG PIZZA

A delicious dessert pizza made with a cinnamon crust, topped with juicy apples, figs and walnuts.

Preparation time: 15 minutes.
Cooking time: 30 minutes.
Makes 1 pizza.

For the cinnamon crust
¾ cup plain flour (maida)
2 tablespoons powdered sugar
½ teaspoon cinnamon powder
3 tablespoons butter

For the topping
3 tablespoons chopped walnuts
½ cup diced apples
5 nos. dried figs, soaked in water and chopped
2 tablespoons honey
½ teaspoon cinnamon powder
1 tablespoon butter
1 teaspoon lemon juice

For the cinnamon crust
1. Combine the flour, sugar and cinnamon in a bowl.
2. Add the butter and rub it into the flour using your fingertips till it resembles breadcrumbs.
3. Add 1 tablespoon of cold water if required and make a firm dough.

4. *Roll out into a circle of 150 mm. (6") diameter and 12.5 mm. (½") thickness and place on a greased baking tray.*
5. *Prick the crust with a fork at regular intervals.*
6. *Refrigerate for 10 to 15 minutes.*
7. *Bake in a preheated oven at 180°C (350°F) for 10 to 12 minutes. Remove the half baked crust from the oven.*

For the topping
1. *Combine all the ingredients for the topping in a bowl, keeping aside 1 tablespoon of walnuts to sprinkle on top.*

How to proceed
1. *Spoon the topping onto the half-baked crust.*
2. *Sprinkle the balance 1 tablespoon of chopped walnuts on top.*
3. *Bake in a preheated oven at 200°C (400°F) for 15 minutes or till the base is crisp.*
4. *Remove from the oven, cool slightly and cut into wedges. Serve warm.*

● *You can also use peaches instead of apples.*

● *You can also use the Sweet Dough recipe on page 13, instead of the cinnamon crust. Just add 1 teaspoon of cinnamon powder to the recipe.*

FRUIT AND ALMOND PIZZAS

A delicious almond pizza base topped with a sweet vanilla flavoured yoghurt and sliced fruits.

Preparation time: 15 minutes.
Cooking time: 20 minutes.
Makes 1 pizza.

For the almond base
1/2 cup plain flour (maida)
3 tablespoons ground almonds
1/2 teaspoon baking powder
3 tablespoons castor sugar
1/4 cup butter
2 tablespoons milk

To be whisked into a topping
1/4 cup thick curds
1/4 cup castor sugar
1/4 cup fresh cream
1 teaspoon vanilla essence

For the garnish
1 cup sliced fruits (oranges, figs, peaches, mangoes, grapes, cherries etc.)
1 teaspoon brown sugar (optional)

Other ingredients
butter or oil for greasing

For the base
1. Mix the flour, almonds and baking powder.
2. Cream the sugar and butter.
3. Add the flour mixture and milk to make a soft dough.
4. Press the dough onto a 150 mm. (6") diameter greased pie dish.
5. Bake in a preheated oven at 180°C (350°F) for 15 to 20 minutes or till golden brown.
6. Remove from the oven, cool completely and unmould from the pie dish.

How to proceed
1. Place the almond base on a serving plate and spread the topping over it.
2. Decorate with fruit slices and brown sugar and chill. Cut into wedges and serve.

● To get thick curds, hang fresh curds in a muslin cloth for 30 minutes and allow the excess liquid to drain out.

VARIATION:
MINI FRUIT AND ALMOND PIZZAS
Picture on page 36
You can make mini pizzas by cutting the dough into small circles using a cookie cutter and then baking them on a greased baking tray. Decorate each one individually as desired using the topping and fruits.

ALL ABOUT PASTA

While the debate continues as to which country deserves credit for inventing pasta, there is no question that the Italians have made them famous.

Pasta is a generic term for many products which are made from a dough of durum wheat flour or semolina. *Here, there are two kinds of pasta - those you can buy and those you must make. A good Italian cook would never hesitate to do both.*

All kinds of dried pasta are commonly referred to as "Macaroni" and this includes all shapes and flavours. They are cooked in water and served with a sauce and sometimes with nothing more than a little butter and a sprinkling of grated cheese.

Fresh or home-made pasta such as ravioli, fettuccine etc. are time consuming to make but the efforts are always worthwhile.

Sorting out the name of a dish from the name of a pasta is impossible as very often they are one and the same. There are so many varieties of fresh and dry pasta that it is easy to be confused as to which variety of pasta goes with a particular sauce. ***Thicker or stuffed pastas are better with robust or thick sauces while thin pastas like spaghetti etc. are better with lighter sauces.*** *There are certain guidelines to follow, but pasta is flexible in more ways than one, so feel free to use any pasta and sauce combination you like!*

Whichever pasta you use, be it fresh or dried pasta, be sure to get the best quality you can.

PASTA

VARIETIES OF PASTA

1. **Alphabet** - *Small alphabet shaped pasta ideally used for soups.*

2. **Angel Hair Pasta (Capelli d' Angelo)** - *Very thin strands of pasta, usually sold in coils.*

3. **Cannelloni** - *Smaller sheets of pasta (like lasagne) that are cooked in water, stuffed with a filling mixture and rolled lightly like a cylinder. These are placed on a baking tray topped with a sauce and baked.*

4. **Conchiglie (Shells)** - *Ridged shaped shells ranging in size from small bite sized shells to large ones.*

5. **Farfalle (Bow ties)** - *Butterfly shaped pasta.*

6. **Fettuccine (Tagliatelle)** - *Long flat ribbon shaped pasta usually about 6 mm. (¼") wide. It is available dried as plain, spinach, tomato or wholewheat fettuccine. It can also be made fresh.*

7. **Fusilli (Spirals)** - *Small pasta in the shape of spindles or corkscrews .*

8. **Lasagne** - *Sheets of fresh or dried pasta, usually cooked layered with filling and sauce and baked. Lasagne sheets can be brought ready-made or can be freshly made. This pasta can be flavoured with a variety of vegetable purées like spinach, tomato, carrot or several fresh or dried herbs or saffron.*

9. **Linguine** - *A flat, strand like pasta, much thinner than fettuccine.*

10. Macaroni - *Long or short cut tubes of pasta which may be ridged or elbow shaped.*

11. Penne - *Short, thick tubes of pasta with diagonal cut ends.*

12. Ravioli - *Fresh pasta which is filled with a sweet or savoury mixture. The filling is encased between 2 sheets of thin pasta which is cooked in water and served with a sauce.*

13. Spaghetti - *Long strands of pasta. These can be fine, medium or thick strands. Spaghetti is the most commonly available pasta.*

14. Tortellini - *Similar to ravioli, but with a twisted irregular shape.*

15. Vermicelli - *Fine slender strands of pasta, which can be long or even small strips.*

Some of these varieties are identified on the picture overleaf.

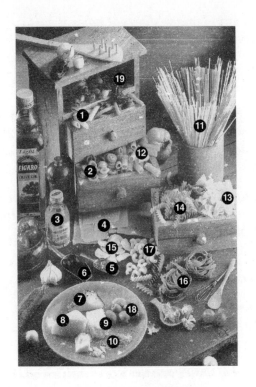

1. Penne
2. Dried Tortellini
3. Olive Oil
4. Dried Lasagne sheets
5. Chilli flakes
6. Black Olives
7. Flavoured cheese
8. Cooking cheese
9. Mozzarella
10. Grated Parmesan cheese
11. Spaghetti
12. Macaroni
13. Farfalle (Bow ties)
14. Fusilli (Spirals)
15. Dried Ravioli
16. Fettuccine
17. Elbow Macaroni
18. Green Olives
19. Sun Dried Tomatoes

HOW TO COOK PASTA

Preparation time : Nil.
Cooking time: 5 to 10 minutes.
Makes 3 cups.

*2 cups dried pasta (penne, spaghetti, fusilli, conchiglie,
fettuccine, macaroni, dried lasagne sheets)*
1 tablespoon oil (for cooking)
1 tablespoon oil (for tossing)
1 teaspoon salt

1. *Boil plenty of water in a large pan with 1 teaspoon of salt
   and 1 tablespoon of oil.*
2. *Add the pasta to the boiling water by adding a few strands
   or one sheet of pasta at a time.*
3. *Cook uncovered, stirring occasionally and gently until the
   pasta is tender. Cooking times may vary with the size and
   the thickness of the pasta. Very small pasta (like macaroni,
   fusilli, conchiglie, penne) may cook in 5 minutes, while
   larger shapes (like spaghetti, fettuccine, dried lasagne
   sheets) may require 10 minutes.*
4. *Immediately drain the cooked pasta into a sieve or a
   colander. Transfer to a bowl of cold water to refresh it.
   Drain again and keep aside.*

Clockwise from top right:
Penne with Celery - Almond Sauce; page 78
Spaghetti with Spinach and Mushrooms; page 74
Whole Wheat Fettucine with Medici Sauce; page 75

5. If the pasta is not to be used immediately, add 1 tablespoon of oil to it and toss it.

- The secret of cooking pasta is to use ample water.

- Cooked pasta should be 'al dente' or "firm to the bite". Undercooked pasta is undesirable and has a taste of raw flour, whereas overcooked pasta will be soft and sticky.

- Generally speaking, fresh pasta will take about 2 to 5 minutes to cook. Fresh pasta does not increase much in volume whilst cooking, as it does not absorb much water.

DO'S AND DONT'S OF PASTA MAKING

- The flour used should be of good quality.

- Certain flours may require a little more oil to knead the dough than mentioned in the recipe.

- When fresh herbs are to be used in the pasta dough, chop them finely.

- If vegetable purées are used, the vegetables should not be discoloured whilst cooking and the purée should be strained before using.

- The pasta dough should be firm and well kneaded.

- Whilst rolling the pasta, care must be taken not to tear the pasta sheet. Also, the pasta should be rolled out as thinly as possible to an almost translucent sheet.

- While rolling the pasta, use cornflour instead of flour for dusting to prevent the pasta from sticking when it is cooked in boiling water.

HOW TO MAKE PASTA

FRESH PASTA DOUGH

A basic pasta recipe to make lasagne, cannelloni, tortellini, ravioli or fettuccine.

Preparation time: 10 minutes.
Cooking time: 10 minutes.
Serves 4.

1 cup plain flour (maida)
4 tablespoons olive oil or oil
1/4 teaspoon salt

How to proceed
1. *Combine all the ingredients in a bowl and knead into a very firm but smooth dough using very little water.*
2. *Rest the dough under a wet muslin cloth for 15 minutes and use as required.*

VARIATIONS:
WHOLE WHEAT PASTA DOUGH:
Use 1/2 cup plain flour (maida) and 1/2 cup whole wheat flour (gehun ka atta) instead of 1 cup plain flour to the above recipe.

VEGETABLE PASTA DOUGH:

Add 2 tablespoons of either tomato, carrot, spinach or beetroot purée to the fresh pasta recipe. You may not require water whilst kneading the dough.

FLAVOURED PASTA DOUGH:

Flavour fresh pasta dough by adding any of the following ingredients to the above recipe :-
1 tablespoon mixed herbs (parsley, thyme, oregano, chilli flakes)
1 tablespoon crushed peppercorns
1 tablespoon garlic paste
8 to 10 saffron strands, rubbed in 1 tablespoon of warm milk

- *For lasagne, the pasta should be rolled to suit the size of the serving dish.*

- *For fettuccine, the pasta sheet should be rolled and cut into 6 mm. (¼") strips.*

PASTA SOUPS AND STARTERS

CORN, BASIL AND FUSILLI SOUP

Picture on page 17

A delicately flavoured soup.

Preparation time : 5 minutes.
Cooking time : 25 minutes.
Serves 4.

1 onion, chopped
2 cloves garlic, chopped
¾ cup cream style sweet corn (canned)
10 basil leaves, chopped
⅓ cup fusilli
1 teaspoon Pesto, page 22
1 teaspoon olive oil or oil
salt and pepper to taste

For the garnish
2 tablespoons grated cheese
basil leaves (optional)

1. Heat the oil and sauté the onion and garlic till the onion is translucent.
2. Add the corn and sauté for one minute.

3. Add 3 cups of water, the basil and fusilli and simmer till the fusilli is cooked.
4. Add the Pesto, salt and pepper and bring to a boil.
   Serve hot, garnished with the cheese and basil leaves.

HERB TORTELLINI SOUP

Picture on page 63

Cheese filled herb tortellinis simmered in a vegetable stew. Though the recipe sounds difficult to make, it is well worth the effort.

Preparation time: 15 minutes.
Cooking time: 30 minutes.
Serves 4.

½ recipe herb tortellini, page 71
½ teaspoon garlic, chopped
1 onion, diced
3 stalks celery, sliced
½ cup carrot, finely chopped
a pinch nutmeg
1 seasoning cube (vegetarian)
1 tablespoon butter
salt to taste

For the garnish
1 teaspoon chopped parsley

1. Make the tortellini as per the recipe but do not cook it in water. Keep aside.
2. Heat the butter in a large pan and sauté the garlic and onion for 1 minute.
3. Add the celery and carrot and sauté till they soften.
4. Add 4 cups of water and simmer till the vegetables are almost cooked.
5. Add the nutmeg, seasoning cube and salt and simmer.
6. Add the uncooked tortellinis and boil for 4 to 5 minutes.

Serve hot garnished with parsley.

SHELL PASTA SALAD WITH PESTO DRESSING

A crunchy salad flavoured with fresh basil.

Preparation time: 10 minutes.
Cooking time: 10 minutes.
Serves 4.

3 cups cooked shell pasta (conchiglie), page 55
½ cup cottage cheese (paneer), cubes

To mixed into a dressing
½ cup walnuts, finely chopped
½ cup basil leaves, chopped
2 tablespoons garlic, grated
3 tablespoons lime juice
5 tablespoons olive oil or salad oil
salt to taste

1. *Mix the shell pasta and cottage cheese and place in the refrigerator.*
2. *Just before serving, toss the pasta in the dressing. Serve chilled.*

PRIMAVERA SALAD

Picture on page 18

An unusual dressing of herb flavoured curds and cream is the highlight of this salad.

Preparation time : 5 minutes.
Cooking time : 5 minutes.
Serves 4.

1½ cups cooked fusilli, page 55
4 cups iceberg lettuce, torn into pieces
½ cup broccoli florets, blanched
¼ cup dried mushrooms, soaked (optional)
4 to 6 asparagus, cut into pieces, blanched
4 cherry tomatoes, halved

Cont'd....

Top: *Tandoori Paneer Calzone; page 39*
Bottom: *Herb Tortellini Soup; page 60*

To be mixed into a dressing

6 tablespoons curds
8 tablespoons cream
4 tablespoons spring onion greens, finely chopped
2 tablespoons celery, finely chopped
salt to taste

1. *Combine all the ingredients in a large bowl and chill.*
2. *Just before serving, add the dressing and toss the salad well.*
   Serve immediately.

- *You can use any vegetable combination of your choice eg. baby corn, snow peas, carrots etc.*
- *After you blanch the vegetables, immerse them in cold water so that they retain their original colour.*

Top: *Herb Tortellini with Garlic Butter; page 71*
Bottom: *Cannelloni Pinwheels with Tomata Cream Sauce; page 66*

PASTA MAIN COURSES

CANNELLONI PINWHEELS WITH TOMATO CREAM SAUCE

Picture on page 64

An attractively presented pasta with a creamy tomato sauce.

Preparation time: 30 minutes.
Cooking time: 30 minutes.
Serves 4.

For the cannelloni
1 recipe fresh pasta dough, page 57
1 tablespoon oil and 1 teaspoon salt to cook the pasta

To be mixed into a paneer filling
1 cup paneer, grated
½ teaspoon chilli flakes
2 teaspoons fresh parsley, chopped
salt to taste

For the spinach filling
2 cups blanched spinach leaves, drained and chopped
2 tablespoons onion, chopped
1 teaspoon green chillies, chopped
½ teaspoon garlic, chopped
2 teaspoons olive oil or oil
salt to taste

For the Tomato Cream Sauce

2 large tomatoes, blanched, deseeded and chopped
2 tablespoons onion, chopped
1 teaspoon garlic, chopped
1 teaspoon chilli powder
1/4 teaspoon dried oregano
1/4 cup fresh cream
1 tablespoon olive oil or oil
salt to taste

For the garnish

4 parsley sprigs

For the cannelloni

1. Divide the dough into 2 portions and roll out each portion as thinly as possible.
2. Cut each portion of the rolled out dough into a 200 mm. x 200 mm. (8" x 8") square.
3. Heat plenty of water in a broad pan and add 1 teaspoon of salt and 1 tablespoon of oil.
4. Drop the prepared pasta one sheet at a time into the boiling water and cook for 2 minutes.
5. Drain and transfer into a bowl of cold water. Drain and keep aside.

For the spinach filling

1. Heat the olive oil in a pan, add the onion, green chillies and garlic and sauté for 2 minutes.
2. Add the spinach and salt, cook for 2 more minutes and keep aside.

For the Tomato Cream Sauce
1. *Heat the olive oil in a pan, add the onion and garlic and sauté for a few minutes.*
2. *Add the tomatoes and cook till the moisture evaporates.*
3. *Add the chilli powder, oregano, cream and salt and mix well.*
4. *Remove from the fire and keep aside.*

For the Cannelloni Pinwheels
1. *Place one cooked pasta sheet on a dry surface. On one half of the sheet, spread half the spinach filling and on the other half, spread half the paneer filling.*
2. *Roll up the pasta tightly, starting from the spinach filling side of the pasta, to make a Swiss Roll.*
3. *Cut the rolled cannelloni into 25 mm. (1") slices. Place the cannelloni slices on a serving dish, placing the cut side upwards to form pinwheels.*
4. *Repeat the same for the other cooked pasta square and the remaining filling to make more pinwheels.*

How to proceed
1. *Place 4 to 6 pinwheels on each serving dish.*
2. *Heat the tomato cream sauce and spoon it carefully over the pinwheels.*
3. *Garnish with parsley and serve immediately.*

**RATATOUILLE
LASAGNE**

**Layers of fresh spinach
lasagne interlaced with a
traditional aubergine
ratatouille and creamy
white sauce.**

Preparation time: 30 minutes.
Cooking time: 1 hour.
Serves 4.

For the spinach lasagne
¾ cup plain flour (maida)
1½ tablespoons spinach purée
3 tablespoons olive oil or oil
¼ teaspoon salt
1 tablespoon oil and 1 teaspoon salt to cook the pasta

For the ratatouille
1 large onion, sliced
¼ cup celery, chopped
2 teaspoons garlic
1½ cups brinjals, diced
1 cup tomatoes, diced
½ teaspoon dried mixed herbs
2 tablespoons tomato ketchup
2 tablespoons olive oil or oil
salt and pepper to taste

For the white sauce
1½ cups milk
1 tablespoon plain flour (maida)
2 tablespoons cheese, grated

2 tablespoons butter
salt and pepper to taste

Other ingredients
½ cup cooking cheese or mozzarella cheese, grated
butter or oil for greasing

For the spinach lasagne
1. Combine all the ingredients in a bowl and knead to a very firm dough, using very little water only if required.
2. Rest the dough under a damp cloth for 15 minutes.
3. Divide into 3 equal portions and roll out each portion as thinly as possible into a circle of 150 mm. (6") diameter.
4. Cook each sheet of lasagne for 2 minutes in a large pan of boiling water to which 1 teaspoon of salt and 1 tablespoon of oil has been added.
5. Drain and transfer the lasange sheets in a bowl of cold water. Drain again and keep aside.

For the ratatouille
1. Heat the oil, add the onion, celery and garlic and sauté for 2 minutes.
2. Add the brinjals and salt and sauté till the brinjals soften.
3. Add the tomatoes and mixed herbs and mix well.
4. When the tomatoes soften, add the ketchup, salt and pepper and mix again. Keep aside.

For the white sauce
1. Heat the butter, add the flour and sauté for 1 minute.
2. Slowly pour in the milk, whisking it continuously so that no lumps form.
3. Add the cheese, salt and pepper and mix well. Remove from the fire.

How to proceed

1. Grease a 150 mm. (6") diameter baking dish.
2. Place one sheet of the spinach lasagne on the baking dish.
3. Top with half the ratatouille and then spoon some white sauce over.
4. Place a second sheet of the spinach lasagne and then spoon the remaining ratatouille and a little of the white sauce over it.
5. Place the third sheet of spinach lasagne and top with the remaining white sauce.
6. Sprinkle the grated cheese on top and bake in a preheated oven at 200°C (400°F) for 10 to 15 minutes or till the cheese browns lightly.

   Serve hot.

HERB TORTELLINI WITH GARLIC BUTTER

Picture on page 64

Herb tortellini stuffed with cheese and tossed with vegetables in garlic butter.

Preparation time: 20 minutes.
Cooking time: 20 minutes.
Makes 35 to 40 tortellinis.

For the herb tortellini

1 cup plain flour (maida)
1 teaspoon dried oregano
1 teaspoon dried thyme
1 teaspoon parsley, chopped
1 teaspoon chilli flakes

71

4 tablespoons olive oil or oil
salt to taste
1 tablespoon oil and 1 teaspoon salt to cook the pasta

For the filling
1 cup cheese, grated

Other ingredients
1 cup finely chopped vegetables (capsicum, carrots, celery etc.)
2 teaspoons garlic, chopped
4 tablespoons butter
salt and pepper to taste

For the herb tortellini
1. Sieve the flour and salt together.
2. Add the oregano, thyme, parsley, chilli flakes and olive oil and knead to a firm dough adding a little cold water if necessary.
3. Cover with a wet muslin cloth and allow it to rest for about 15 minutes.
4. Divide the dough into two portions and roll out each portion as thinly as you can without breaking the sheet.
5. Using a 50 mm. (2") diameter cookie cutter, cut into circles.
6. Place ¼ teaspoon of the cheese in little heaps in the centre of each circle.
7. Brush the sides of the circle with a little cold water and fold it into a semicircle sealing the edges.
8. Brush the corners of the semicircle with cold water and join them together by pressing the edges firmly (refer to diagram).
9. Cook the tortellini for 3 to 4 minutes in a large pan of boiling water to which 1 teaspoon of salt and 1 tablespoon of oil has been added.

10. *Drain and transfer the herb tortellini into a bowl of cold water. Drain again and keep aside.*

How to proceed

1. *Heat the butter in a saucepan, add the garlic and sauté for a few seconds.*
2. *Add the vegetables, salt and pepper and sauté.*
3. *Add the cooked herb tortellini and toss gently. Serve immediately.*

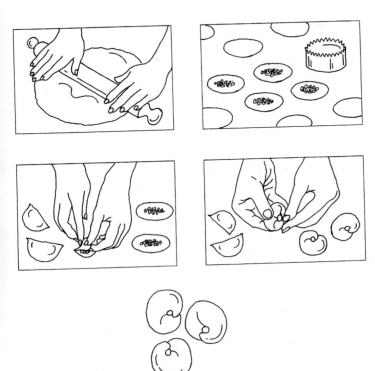

SPAGHETTI WITH SPINACH AND MUSHROOMS
Picture on page 54

A wholesome pasta dish tossed with spinach and fresh mushrooms.

Preparation time: 10 minutes.
Cooking time: 10 minutes.
Serves 4.

3 cups cooked spaghetti, page 55

For the sauce
1 cup fresh spinach, blanched, drained and chopped
1 cup mushrooms, blanched and sliced
1 tablespoon garlic, chopped
2 spring onions, chopped
½ cup fresh cream
4 tablespoons grated cheese
½ cup milk
1 tablespoon olive oil or oil
salt and pepper to taste

For the garnish
2. *tablespoons tomato pieces*

For the sauce
1. *Heat the olive oil, add the garlic and spring onions and sauté for 2 minutes.*
2. *Add the spinach, mushrooms, cream, milk, cheese, salt and pepper and allow the sauce to simmer for 5 minutes.*
3. *Remove from the fire and keep hot.*

74

How to proceed

1. *Just before serving, toss the spaghetti gently in the sauce till it is well coated.*
   Serve hot, garnished with tomato pieces.

Note:

You can use a combination of plain flour and whole wheat flour spaghetti as shown in the picture on page 54.

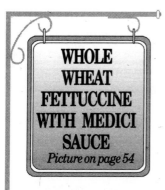

WHOLE WHEAT FETTUCCINE WITH MEDICI SAUCE
Picture on page 54

A nutritious pasta with a spicy tomato sauce.

Preparation time: 10 minutes.
Cooking time: 30 minutes.
Serves 3 to 4.

1 recipe fresh whole wheat pasta dough, page 57
1 tablespoon oil and 1 teaspoon salt to cook the pasta

For the Medici sauce

1½ cups tomato pulp
1 tablespoon garlic, chopped
2 spring onions, chopped
1 tablespoon chilli flakes
1 teaspoon chilli powder
2 tablespoons tomato purée
4 tablespoons fresh cream
2 tablespoons olive oil or oil
salt to taste

For the garnish

4 tablespoons grated cheese
1 tablespoon spring onion greens, chopped
8 black olives, deseeded (optional)

For the whole wheat fettuccine

1. Divide the pasta dough into 2 portions and roll out each portion as thinly as possible.
2. Cut each portion of the rolled out dough into a 200 mm. x 200 mm. (8" x 8") square.
3. Roll up the pasta sheet and cut into 6 mm. (1/4") strips.
4. Heat plenty of water in a broad pan and add 1 teaspoon of salt and 1 tablespoon of oil. Add a few strands of the fettuccine to the boiling water at a time and cook for 2 to 3 minutes.
5. Drain and transfer into a bowl of cold water. Drain again and keep aside.

For the Medici sauce

1. Heat the olive oil, add the garlic and spring onions and sauté for 1 minute.
2. Add the tomato pulp and cook till the sauce thickens.
3. Add the chilli flakes, chilli powder, tomato purée, salt and ½ cup of water and bring to a boil.
4. Add the cream. Mix well and keep aside.

How to proceed

1. Just before serving, re-heat the Medici sauce and toss the whole wheat fettuccine in it
2. Serve hot, garnished with the cheese, spring onion greens and black olives.

● Tomato pulp is made by blanching whole tomatoes in hot water and thereafter peeling, deseeding and chopping them.

BOW PASTA WITH SUN-DRIED TOMATO PESTO SAUCE

Pasta with a rich and creamy sun-dried tomato pesto sauce.

Preparation time: 15 minutes.
Cooking time: 15 minutes.
Serves 4.

3 cups cooked bow pasta (farfalle), page 55
½ cup cheese, grated

For the sauce
1 recipe sun-dried tomato pesto, page 23
1 cup fresh cream
1 cup milk
salt to taste

For the sauce
1. *Put the sun-dried tomato pesto, fresh cream, milk and salt in a large saucepan and allow it to simmer for 3 to 4 minutes.*
2. *Remove from the fire and keep hot.*

How to proceed
1. *Just before serving, heat the sauce and toss the pasta in it.*
2. *Garnish with cheese and serve hot.*

PENNE WITH CELERY-ALMOND SAUCE
Picture on page 54

Penne with a creamy mustard, celery and almond sauce.

Preparation time: 10 minutes.
Cooking time: 15 minutes.
Serves 4.

3 cups cooked penne, page 55

For the sauce
1 large onion, sliced
½ cup celery, sliced
2 teaspoons plain flour (maida)
2 cups milk
¼ cup cream
½ cup grated cheese
¼ cup chopped almonds, toasted
¾ teaspoon French style mustard
3 tablespoons butter
salt and pepper to taste

For the sauce
1. *Heat the butter and sauté the onion and celery for a few minutes.*
2. *Add the flour, mix well and stir for 1 minute.*
3. *Gradually add the milk, mixing well so that lumps do not form.*
4. *Add the cream, cheese, almonds, mustard, salt and pepper, mix well and allow it to simmer for 3 to 4 minutes.*
5. *Remove from the fire and keep warm.*

How to proceed

Toss the penne into the sauce just before serving and mix well.
Serve hot.

● *You can add some milk or water if you want a thinner*
   sauce.

SHELL PASTA WITH CREAMY MUSHROOM SAUCE

**A delicately flavoured
mushroom sauce served
with shell pasta
(conchiglie).**

Preparation time : 15 minutes.
Cooking time : 15 minutes.
Serves 4.

3 cups cooked shell pasta (conchiglie), page 55
½ cup cheese, grated

For the sauce
3 cups mushrooms, thickly sliced
3 onions, sliced
2 teaspoons garlic, chopped
2 tablespoons plain flour (maida)
3 cups milk
¼ cup fresh cream
5 tablespoons butter
salt and pepper to taste

For the sauce

1. Heat the butter in a large saucepan, add the onions and garlic and cook for some time.
2. Add the mushrooms and flour and cook for a further 3 to 4 minutes.
3. Add the milk gradually, mixing well to make sure no lumps form. Bring to a boil.
4. Add the fresh cream, salt and pepper and keep aside.

How to proceed

1. Just before serving, re-heat the sauce, adding a little milk or water if required, and toss the pasta in it.
2. Serve hot, garnished with the cheese.

● *If you like, brandy can be added at step 4 to flavour this sauce.*

PENNE WITH CREAMY VEGETABLES

A simple and delicious recipe.

Preparation time: 10 minutes.
Cooking time: 15 minutes.
Serves : 4.

3 cups cooked penne, page 55
1 teaspoon garlic
1/3 cup snow peas (mangetout), cleaned and blanched
1/3 cup broccoli florets, blanched
1/3 cup fresh green asparagus, cut into 25 mm. (1") pieces
   and blanched
1 seasoning cube (vegetarian), crumbled.
1 1/2 cups fresh cream
1/3 cup cheese, grated
3 tablespoons olive oil
salt and pepper to taste

1. *Heat the olive oil, add the garlic and sauté for a few seconds.*
2. *Add the snow peas, broccoli, asparagus, seasoning cube, cream and salt and cook for 2 minutes.*
3. *Add the penne and cook for a further 2 minutes until the penne is evenly coated with the sauce.*
4. *Remove from the fire, sprinkle the cheese on top and serve hot.*

● *Make this dish as close to serving time as possible.*

EGGPLANT AND MACARONI CAKE

A tasty baked pasta preparation.

Preparation time: 15 minutes.
Cooking time: 30 minutes.
Serves 4.

For the eggplant layer
1 large eggplant (brinjal), thinly sliced
1 tablespoon plain flour (maida)
¼ teaspoon crushed pepper
2 tablespoons olive oil or oil
salt to taste

For the pasta layer
1½ cups cooked macaroni, page 55
½ cup tomato sauce, page 20
4 tablespoons cheese, grated
1 tablespoon tomato ketchup
1 tablespoon chilli sauce
1 teaspoon fresh basil, chopped
salt to taste

To be mixed into a topping
4 tablespoons bread crumbs
2 tablespoons butter

Other ingredients

oil for greasing

For the eggplant layer

1. *Sieve the flour and salt together. Add in the crushed pepper.*
2. *Coat each slice of eggplant with the flour mixture.*
3. *Heat the oil in a large pan and cook the eggplant slices on a slow flame on both sides till the slices are evenly browned. Drain and keep aside.*

For the pasta layer

Mix together all the ingredients in a bowl and keep aside.

How to proceed

1. *Grease a 200 mm. x 200 mm. (8" x 8") baking dish.*
2. *Line the baking dish with half of the eggplant slices placing them close to one another ensuring there are no gaps.*
3. *Spoon in the pasta mixture on top of the eggplant layer.*
4. *Place the remaining eggplant slices on top of the pasta.*
5. *Cover with the bread crumbs and butter topping.*
6. *Bake in a preheated oven at 200°C (400°F) for 20 minutes till the bread crumbs are evenly browned.*

- *You can add ½ cup of boiled vegetables (baby corn, french beans, carrot) to the pasta mixture to make a nutritious alternative.*

BOW PASTA WITH CURRIED VEGETABLES

Bow-tie pasta tossed with vegetables in a curry powder flavoured sauce.

Preparation time: 10 minutes.
Cooking time: 15 minutes.
Serves 4.

1½ cups cooked bow pasta (farfalle), page 55
1 clove garlic, chopped
1 onion, chopped
¼ cup celery, chopped
4 to 5 tomatoes, blanched, deseeded and chopped
1 cup sliced baby corn, blanched
½ cup fresh mushrooms, sliced
½ cup capsicum, blanched and diced
2 tablespoons Madras curry powder
1 tablespoon butter
salt to taste

1. *Heat the butter in a saucepan and sauté the garlic, onion and celery for a few minutes.*
2. *Add the tomatoes and simmer for 5 to 7 minutes.*
3. *Add the pasta, baby corn, mushrooms, capsicum, Madras curry powder and salt and stir on a low flame till the tomatoes coat the pasta and vegetables.*
   Serve hot.